QUEEN AL-NISA

POETRY FROM A TEENAGER'S MIND

C. Watkins

QUEEN AL-NISA: Poetry From a Teenager's Mind
July 31, 2022
C. Watkins
ISBN# 978-1-953526-12-0

Published by TaylorMade Publishing
Jacksonville, FL
www.TaylorMadePublishingFL.com
(904) 323-1334

TaylorMade Publishing

Table of Contents

Introduction

This poetry book was created from the thoughts of the teenage version of myself. When we are young, we show a lot of self-expression. We become very creative with our feelings and choose the path of telling our stories through writing, art, music, or dance. Most teens never want to straightforwardly talk about what they are feeling, and it takes others to read between the lines of their art to learn the truth.

Having a type of emotional release to transfer the energy from our thoughts into another form, allows us to understand ourselves and process our emotions. When we acknowledge our feelings instead of denying them, we alleviate stress and anxiety, boost our self-esteem, and even fight depression. I hope you will feel my love, pain, and growth throughout these words and find a way to express yourself to the world.

Love or Lust

Please Don't Go

Please don't go
I can't take the pain
The fact that you might be gone
Is driving me insane
My love for you is deep
As deep as the ocean blue
No one can ever beat
The love I have for you
I called you this morning
To make sure you were okay
But when I called you were gone
It took my breath away
I thought about you all night
All the way to the day
My tears put up a fight
But I told myself I'd be ok
My thoughts worried me
I wondered what you were going through
Were you also thinking about me
The way I was thinking about you
Baby I love you so much
I want to be your wife
I can't wait to feel your touch
I'll always be in your life
I'm praying for you my love
That's all you need to know
God is watching you from above
So baby please don't go

First Sight

Everything is dark around me
I feel this tickling up my body
But it isn't pain
I don't know what it is
Am I insane
There's a voice calling me
His voice is soft and sweet
I feel his fingers touch me
He leaves my body at ease
He whispers in my ear
And says lovely things
He makes me feel warm
Even when I feel rain
As I open my eyes
I see the person that has spoken
To me every day and night
That left my heart unbroken
I told him I had a secret
A secret I could not say
But if he thought he had known
Would he whisper in my ear and tell me
He told me love at first sight
Is what I feel
And he knows from the bottom of his heart
That it's true
And that it's real
So I asked him again
Does he feel the same way I do
Cause I need to know
That what I feel
If he does too

The Lovely You

The lovely you
The one I miss
The lovely you
Would steal a kiss
But who would think
You being so smart
You stole something I loved
You stole my heart
The lovely you
Oh how I miss your sweet smell
That everybody would inhale
I miss the lovely words you would say
That easily took my breath away
But yet
I don't miss what you did to me
You put me in tears
Took the life from me
And then
You come back with words today
That don't even express the way
I feel inside
But our love can't deny
The way I feel boo
Cause oh how I miss
The lovely you

My One and Only You

My one and only life
My one and only you
My one and only dream
Finally came true
I prayed day and night
To find someone like you
And Jesus was right
I had to do what I had to do
You're my one and only love
My one and only thought
You're the one from above
The one Jesus brought
You give me a kiss
Upon my sexy lips
And you make sure you don't miss
So you grab hold of my hips
You tell me you love me
You tell me you care
You tell me you'll never leave me
And that you'll always be there
So you're my one and only
And I am yours too
From deep down in my heart
I'll do anything for you

Together We Stand

We will be together
Through thick and thin
We will never be separated
We'll be together to the end
We will stand together
No matter how hard it gets
We will be happy together
With no regrets
We will stay together
I promise you that
No if and or buts
And that's a fact
We will die together
Having the best memories in mind
I'll always remember
You were one of a kind

Later On

One day we'll be together
Later on is what I mean
I want to get married and have kids
That's how our life should be
We're gonna be together for life
That's my plan you see
You need to tell me you'll be my life
And that we will always be
Boy I love you so much
You are my heart and soul
I love that wonderful touch
You make my heart whole
You're the only individual
That can understand me
Your healing is sexual
And you don't hear complaining out of me
So later on in life
We'll be the best in the world
Because you are my man
And I am your girl

Unforgettable Love

Things happen to people
For many different reasons
It hurts inside
But only one can please them
When a relationship ends
For some females it's hard to mend
That's why their hearts are filled with sorrow
Never looking forward
To the good in tomorrow
Her mind is set
On the one thing she'll never forget
She loved a person
That stole her heart
He took her heart
All the way from the start
He was everything she wished for
But that oncoming fate
She could not endure
That's what made her
Hate life even more
For some people
Love comes and goes
For others
It's real
And you can tell, 'cause it shows
So to sum it all up
All the pain from above
Ended her sweet life
Because she lost her
Unforgettable love

Remembering You

Remembering you
Was a dream come true
I thought I lost you
When you found someone new
Day and night
I tried to remember your name
I thought I was right
But I was wrong again
I looked at your picture
Studied it hard
The more I tried
You put up your guard
Then all of a sudden
It just came to mind
It was your name
It came just in time
It was fun
Trying to remember you
But in the end
You forgot me too

When We First Met

When we first met
I'll never forget
The look that we shared
So intense, so scared
We didn't know what to do
In our minds this is true
In our hearts, just the same
Not enough love, just pain
We talked for a while
Shared some dreams
Told some stories
So compatible it seemed
Just a friend
We tell everyone
But the friendship we have
Has just begun
It'll never end
You wonder how
We share the love, the truth, even a smile
So now you know
The first sight was the best
But the question remains
Did we pass the test

What We Have

What we have is a dream
A piece of fantasy people wish they could have
Most people wouldn't understand the possibilities we bring
The love, the joy, the melody our bodies sing
Time will tell the truth, between life and misery
Eternity spells the love that we share
No rapper, no singer could ever compare
Emotions stir up my feelings for you
There's a multitude of it built between us two
The concept of love has expanded
We French kiss betwixt two lips
So infatuated by your love, I don't know how to handle it
Your words inspire me, make me feel invincible
Your touch, the warmth of you, leaves me at ease
To watch you walk away would bring me down to my knees
Just for you to speak the words
You know I love to hear
Often on my own, I break down into tears
My heart is overwhelmed, by the love you give out
The Passion, The Struggle, I CRY OUT!

Unconditionally

I love you unconditionally
That's what my man tells me
I want to get married and have kids
That's how our lives should be
True love is within you
Deep down in your heart
A heart that he kept with him
Ever since the start
Do you really love me
Do you really care
Do you really have feelings for me
And will you always be there
I love you so much
Baby I do
Please tell me you believe me
Please tell me it's true
Our love is unconditional
That's all I want it to be
Because I know I love you
I just hope you love me

The Boy

He looks, he stares
I give him a glance
Out of the corner of my eye
Wondering if I should give him a chance
He sits beside me
Barely talking, he never speaks
What's going through his head
Is it me?
A nice, charming guy
I wonder why, he keeps to himself
Then it hits me
He's with someone else
That's why he's so calm and doesn't flirt
He has a girl, he doesn't want to hurt

Hate and

Betrayal

Heart Broken

I fell in love with you
And then you broke my heart
I knew never to love a player
I was wrong from the start
Loving you was like
Ripping out my heart
I refused to look around me and see
All the terrible things you were doing to me
I was in my own world, and I didn't see
All the trouble you were
I was deeply in love
Now that's all ruined you see
All because you played me
You had looks, you had charm
You were slick with your words
You knew just what to say
I was foolish to think
We were made for each other
I always prayed
You would never love another
I wanted us to always be with each other
Loving a player
Is the hardest thing ever
I have learned a lot
From my experiences with you
My heart was broken in two
I know now, as I look back on my past
Dating a player would never last
So in the future, I'll watch what I do
I won't date another player
But I'll still always love you

How Could This Happen to Me

Why
Why me
Is it something I did
Please somebody tell me
I did everything right
I didn't cheat
So why is everybody leaving me
I tried to call every night
Walk you to your class
You put up a fight
I thought it would last
But wrong
Wrong I am
I can't keep a relationship
It comes and goes as fast as it can
Is it me or is it you
Is it us
Please tell me what to do
Why am I cursed
Is it something I did
Or worse
Is it something I said
Tell me why
Why me
Because it's too blurry
For my eyes to see

I Never Thought

I never thought
It would be like this
I never thought I'd lose your kiss
I never thought
It would be this hard
Just to get a valentine's card
I never thought
In my life
That you wouldn't want me to be your wife
I thought you loved me
I thought you cared
But I never thought
You wouldn't be there
I never thought
Now I write
That me and you wouldn't be so tight
I always thought
That we would be
But I never thought
That you would leave me

Never Again

Never again
Will I fall for your tricks
But I'm gonna let you know
You got the game mixed
You messed with the wrong girl
I think it's time that you know
But let me make it clear for you
Payback is a mother bro
You think you slick
Tryna play me for a fool
Tryna impress your boys
Dude you not cool
But never again I'll tell you now
I'll never fall for any boy's tricks
I'll show you how
Just try me if you want to
You'll see what I mean
I'll put you out your misery
Leave you on a red beam
Make you go crazy
To think you could ever leave me
But never again
Never again I say
Because all of my love
Has fallen away

Through it All

Through it all
I know that I'll be ok
Even though you put me through so much
Every single day
I tried to put up with you
But I guess it didn't work
So you lead me to think
You wanted me to hurt
You must know me very well
How easy it was for me to tell
You did the stupidest thing in the world
You ran off with another girl
You think this is a game
So you went and tried to cheat
But for all you know
I already got you beat
But through it all
I don't have to tell you again
That in my relationships
I will always win!

Mixed Feelings

Feelings are the hardest things
I've ever dealt with in my life
It's like you're always wrong
Even when it feels so right
Love is a feeling
That people often share
Love is also a feeling
That many people cannot bear
Feelings are eternal
They will never end
They'll be with you when you die
They'll be with you when he comes again
Being scared is a feeling
Being lost and confused is too
Telling people you love them when you don't
Is a feeling that most people are used to

A Lost Love

I once was in love
With this handsome young man
We had our own kind of love
That no one could understand
We used to always argue
Always fuss and fight
But we always found time
To say I love you every night
I miss the way he hugged me
I miss the way he kissed me
I missed the way he touched me
My heart feels so empty
My love for him
Was a dream come true
My heart was broken
When he found someone new
I can't explain the way I feel
Because some people think
It's not a big deal
I lost the one I loved
The one I cared for
Should I take him back
Or not think of him anymore

For I Am

For I am a bright star in the night sky
A beautiful bird that soars up high
I am the thoughts trapped in your mind
That makes you smile every time
But what am I not?
A rug for your feet
Something you walk on as a treat
A toy you buy or a game you play
I am not the one to be messed with, Okay!
My life is hard and times are rough
And right now, I have no time for your stuff
You did me wrong, you played me cheap
My love for you is obsolete

I Don't Want to Say Goodbye

I don't want to say goodbye
To the things that we once had
I'm confused and I hate myself
For making a good thing go bad
I don't want to say goodbye
To the times that we once shared
I can't bear leaving
If you never knew, I truly and deeply cared
I can't seem to say goodbye
And I dread the oncoming end
I know that I have broken something
That this time just won't mend
Do you want to say goodbye
And forget what I may say
Because if that will make you happy
I won't try and make you stay
But I'll never say goodbye
What's in my heart will always stay true
And the truth that will live on forever
Is my undying love for you

Complex Decisions

The strain from this pain I feel
Is driving me insane
The enormous hit it gives my heart
Could stop the rain
The thoughts in my mind, so scrambled
So confused, it makes me feel like an animal
Out of control, unstable to the point
Where I'm intangible
My love for thee shines as bright as the sun
Until this complex, confused stage begun
I hide the feelings I really feel
Until I take the time for my heart to heal
What should I do?
I asked myself at times
Does the person I care for
Have the same love as mine
Confused! Why am I
I want to hit the floor
Be buried in the ground and die
Just tell me why
Why do I cry?
Why do I try?
Why do I care?
Why Do I?

Never Be

We could never be
As bad as that sounds
I can't do anything about it
But cry or make a frown
The feelings that we share
So deep and so true
Can never be progressed
Because of her, because of you
The thoughts in my mind
The nightly dreams
The love in my heart
That can never be seen
The kiss on my lips
The chill up my spine
The way you touch me
Takes control of my mind
To think that we could
Actually be together
Oh, that's just a joke
NEVER!

Life

Life

We take life for granted
Never thinking about what we do
Never paying attention to life itself
Yes, everyone knows it's true
The time we spend arguing
Trying to fuss and fight
There's someone out there dying
Every day and night
To lie and to cheat
Is far from my mind
Leaving all the dangers of the world
As far behind
Life is a precious treasure
One that you're willing to lose
No one could ever measure
To the life you plan to choose
Until the time for death comes
Life is your world
Everything around you is done
You end up in a twirl
You think it's a dream
It can't be reality
You say what does this mean
And since
You don't understand
You will die constantly

Misunderstood Man

Problems, headache, pain
All these things drive him insane
Time comes, time goes
Where he ends up, he'll never know
He has not me, he has not you
He has no one to pull him through
The cracks of life
He's living in
The streets where the hate don't mend
The thoughts in his mind
The shattered dreams
The tears on his pillow
No one's ever seen
The words he speaks
Come straight from his soul
He puts it in his music
It makes him feel whole
He tells his life story
The story he wishes would end
Then start over and begin again
Repeatedly he yells
To let out the fear
That usually turns
Right back to tears
He needs someone to be there
With all their love and all their might
I hope it's not too late
To fix this man's life

What If...

What if I could fly
Like a bird or a plane in the rain
Dig under the earth like a crane
Is it sane or inhumane
I can't help what I think
Who is to blame
Blame the people who criticize and jeopardize
Commits suicide, want to ride or die
Hey I wonder why
Why do things go the way they do
Time goes by right before your eyes
All you hear is lies, just want to die
Turn around and cry and you still wonder why
Hum…
Well…
What if you could stop the time
Take a moment and unwind, clear your mind
Undo that crooked line and stop the crime
You'll be number one this time
Just think about it
life is just a test
To release some stress
To do your best
To past the test
To get your rest
That's my guess
So what is the question
Is life just a gift
To uplift just a myth
That you're with
Maybe
What if

Lost

I am so lost
In this confusing world
I have nowhere to go
I'm left in a twirl
It always seems to me
That my life has no meaning
But as the time passed
I see why I'm leaning
I try too hard to impress
The wrong kind of people
When I should be worshiping God
Because through them he can see through
If I actually take the time
To make everyone understand
I'll be falling in the hands
Of the wrong man
God is who I'm seeking
The devil is whom I'm pleasing
But my family is the one
Who gave me a reason
To go out and do
What I do today
Take the time to change my life
But it still hurts in the end
Because I feel I'm going the wrong way
I guess I'm seeking past what I need

Me

Sitting quietly
Staring into the sky
Picturing if my body could fly
Wondering how my life's gone past me by
Then the understanding of my being is brought to light
I'm needed here to help others feel bright
To lead the way is my goal
To make everyone's soul feel whole
But what about mine
Just because I smile do you think I'm fine
I hide behind the truth inside
I don't take the time to unwind
I need to clear my mind
See where I stand in line
I just have to find the time

Figuratively Speaking

Figuratively speaking
The point of life is death
Am I not correct?
People are here to make the right choices
But sometimes they forget
They live for the world
And the things that it holds
Not doing what God intended for them to do
Do you think you know?
I suppose
Fidelity is in their minds
And not their hearts
Is that they pursue
It sounds great but it is not
You can't just think
You have to do

What's Going On

What's going on in this world today
Kids don't want to learn, they just want to play
Or stay in the streets all night and day
Man, what's going on
Are the teachers not teaching well
Why can't the children read or spell
The child will fail or end up in jail
Man, what's going on
I tried to teach this boy right
I tried with all my might
Then he went in the streets and got in a fight
Man, what's going on
You try to give them respect
But they always reject
The time you give and forget
But they never seem to listen
Want to know what they're missing
Always up in somebody's business
Man, what's going on
Being a fool
Thinking they're cool
Never coming to school
Huh…
They'll be lying in their own drool
Man, what's going on
But all I can say, is that you pray day and night
And hope that you're saved
So that your name, doesn't make it to the grave
Man, what's going on
And on that funny day
You think your fears went away
But for all you know you're dead
Got blood shooting from your head
Man, what's going on
Not to go tell his momma
And all your homeboys fled

[33]

But just to go holla
At a dude they know
Just for show
To brag about what they did
You were just a kid
But they blast those guys back
After they brought that new gat
Man, what's going on
And at the funeral that played your song
You don't know what went wrong
And now you're long gone
Man, what's really going on?

Sophisticated

Is a woman less than a man
Because she does not wear the pants
Or do we misunderstand the fact that a man
Does not stand above us, but right beside us
A woman can take charge and be the boss
But for some individuals
It is hard to adjust to things unfamiliar
The assumption that one can't be sophisticated
Is the idiocy of man
For a woman is not fictitious but noticeably effulgent
My mind tells me that I can see
As far as the galaxy expands
My mind tells me that I can be an educated woman and
Become the next president of the United States
My mind tells me that I am powerful beyond measure, but
The man…
The man tells me that I'm nothing but his whore
I'm sophisticated enough to educate myself
And become as strong as he is
But he is wrong…
He is wrong,
Because I know a woman is more than a slave to a man
I know that a woman is intelligent and capable to be
All that she strives to be
I Am a Woman! Sophisticated

I Wonder Why

I wonder why people don't think about what they have until it's gone
Do they think their love is forever
And no one else can have none
I wonder why they always fight
And the females always cry
The man walks out and never explains why
I wonder why when a man cheats
He's extra special to his girl
And he knows her friends were all around
Ready to tell his every move and twirl
I wonder why a man acts different
When he is around his friends and boys
He knows his girl don't do that
No games or no toys
I wonder why when a female lies
She is always right
And her man gets mad and ready to fight
I wonder why couples don't protect each other
They need to care for one another
And even when they first met
They were willing to forgive and forget
But now it's kind of different
It's like they're both on a mission
To catch each other in the wrong
And they know they're both strong
I wonder why
I wonder why
I wonder why

Reflection

Writing this poetry book has taken me on a journey through my past - a past I thought I would remember because it's about me. I was wrong. Reading the words of such a vulnerable girl is breathtaking. To know I was once her and felt so many emotions kind of took me by surprise.

Thinking how as adults, we tell children their feelings for their peers are not real; it's just puppy love. Yet, I felt everything this younger version of me was going through. No, I do not remember who these were written for. Nor do I feel the pain and confusion that I felt at that time. But I can sympathize with her feelings and know that at that time in life, all those emotions were real.

If I could leave you with one piece of advice it would be this: Stay true to yourself and know that one day you will grow up and you will look at life differently. For now, your life is your life and what you feel matters.

About the Author

For as long as she can remember, Chelsea Watkins has had the ability to speak the right words, at the right time, in just about any situation. As one who has been blessed with the gift of words and declaring her truth, Ms. Watkins's mission is to speak life into people's dreams, encouragement to the discouraged, and love to the brokenhearted.

By sharing these poignant poems written when she was a teenager, Ms. Watkins now adds author to her list of accomplishments, which include mother, teacher, foster parent, entrepreneur, crafter, and motivational speaker.

www.ingramcontent.com/pod-product-compliance
Lightning Source LLC
Chambersburg PA
CBHW070955120626
46546CB00004B/1633